Hugo's Restaurant Cookbook

**Gluten Free, Soy Free, Cow Milk Dairy Free
Easy to Make Healthy and Delicious Recipes**

Teri Sahm & Hugo Tapia Rodriguez

DEDICATION

We dedicate this cookbook to our customers who continually inspire us to create healthy and delicious food that is organic, grass fed, wild, gluten free, soy free, cow milk dairy free, sustainable, good for people and the planet.

CONTENTS

ABOUT OUR RECIPES

Eating and cooking gluten free is getting easier thanks to increased awareness which continually drives more options to the marketplace. If you are diagnosed as gluten intolerant or celiac, it can be daunting at first. But if you take a few deep breaths and start looking at what is available vs. what you can't have, you will begin to see a different way of eating and cooking.

At our restaurant we work with high quality ingredients, preferably as much organic as possible. We avoid GMOs (genetically modified organisms). We continually push our suppliers to broaden their offerings. We would also encourage you to make those same choices at home. Minimizing your exposure to chemicals in your food as well as at home, and avoiding GMO's are an excellent part of a strategy for good health.

When making these recipes at home, there may be some slight variations in cooking time between your oven temperatures and ours. We use commercial equipment in the kitchen, and there is a difference in the power, size and efficiency. This is especially true with regard to blending. You will want to use your most powerful blender for best results.

The last caveat is regarding olive oil. For cooked dishes, we do not use extra virgin olive oil in our recipes. We use olive oil which is milder in flavor. If you use an Extra Virgin Olive Oil (EVOO), then it will change the flavor profile of the recipe. This is neither bad nor good, but it is a personal preference. The World's Healthy Foods Website (www.whfoods.com), recommends never cooking with EVOO, and only using it in salads or items that are not cooked.

We thank you for your interest in our recipes and wish you a prosperous and healthy life!

Signature crackers with sweet potato hummus

1 • SEATED AT THE TABLE

Our signature cracker recipe was developed to be available for guests when seated at our table. Providing something to eat immediately helps ground them and take the edge off their hunger. We serve them with a dipping sauce, currently a sweet potato hummus. Our crackers are much loved by our customers: new and regular.

Teri's Cracker Recipe
Makes 1½ cookie sheets

Ingredients

1 cup Coconut Milk
3 tsp Baking Powder
¾ cup Flour (We use Pamela's Bread Mix)
2 ¼ cups ground brown Flax seed
4 Tbsp Olive Oil or Sunflower Nut Oil
Salt to taste

Directions

1. Measure milk into a bowl and add baking powder. Whisk and let set for 10 minutes to activate.

2. Add flour, salt and flax seed. Mix well.

3. Add oil and mix well again.

4. Grease a cookie sheet.

5. Place dough on cookie sheet and spread it out. Sprinkle salt on top.

6. You can score the dough into squares to make it easier to break uniformly.

7. Bake at 350 for 25 minutes or until done.

Sweet Potato Hummus
Makes about 5 cups

Ingredients

4 Sweet Potatoes, chunky sliced and boiled skin on
1 peeled Orange
1 Bell Pepper
1 stalk Celery
1 tsp ground Cumin
Salt to taste

Directions

1. Boil sweet potatoes until soft. Drain potatoes from water, but retain 1-2 cups of water to use during blending.

2. Slice bell pepper and celery and place in food processor.

3. Peel orange and place in food processor.

4. Continue processing these ingredients until they are finely chopped.

5. Add ½ of sweet potatoes and mix together. You may need to add some of the potato water. Add the rest of the potatoes and mix.

6. Transfer to a blender. Puree mixture until smooth. Add potato water as necessary. Add salt to taste.

Crab cakes

2 • APPETIZERS

Having gluten free Crab Cakes on our menu is a dream come true for our gluten intolerant and celiac friends. Many of them tell us that they haven't had Crab Cakes for 10 years! It is with great joy that we offer this recipe to the Celiac and Gluten Intolerant community.

Crab Cake
Makes about 15 4 oz. crab cakes

Ingredients

2 lbs Wild Crab meat
1 Onion, finely diced
2 stalks Celery, finely diced
2 Tbsp minced Parsley
¾ cup Egg Replacer
2 Tbsp Olive Oil
1 cup gluten-free Breadcrumbs

Directions

1. Heat 1 Tbsp olive oil in sauté pan. Add onion, celery and sauté until soft. Add S & P. Remove from heat and let cool.

2. In a bowl, place cooled onion, celery, parsley. Pulse the crabmeat in a food processor first, to break up the meat. Add the crab to the bowl and mix well so that the ingredients are well incorporated.

3. Add egg replacer and mix well again.

4. Set up a bowl filled with breadcrumb. Take a small portion of crab mixture and roll into the breadcrumb until covered and shape into a cake. Repeat for all crab cakes.   (Continued on next page)

5. When you are ready to cook the crab cakes, place 1 Tbsp of oil in a sauté pan and heat.

6. When the oil is hot, place crab cake on one side to sear until golden, and then sear the other side.

7. Finish in a 400 degree oven by cooking for 3-4 minutes depending on the size.

Crab Mixture   Rolling crab cake in breadcrumb

Protein Bites
Makes 1-2 servings

Ingredients

4 oz of protein (beef, chicken, prawn, fish) cut into bite sized pieces, except for the prawns which can be cooked whole.
1 Tbsp Olive Oil
1 ½ Tbsp Garlic
½ tsp Red Pepper flake
Salt and Pepper to taste

Directions

1. Add oil to the pan and heat. Add garlic and cook until golden.

2. Season the protein with salt and pepper. Add protein and red pepper flake to pan and cook until done.

3. We plate this on a bed of organic greens and serve it with our dairy free, nut free pesto, which follows.

Dairy Free, Nut Free Pesto
Makes about 3 cups

Ingredients

½ lb Basil
1 cup Water
1 cup Olive Oil
Salt and Pepper to taste

Directions

1. Rough chop and puree basil and water until basil is well incorporated in a blender.

2. Slowly drizzle olive oil as you are blending until sauce is complete. Taste and adjust seasoning as needed.

Protein bites with pesto

Flatbread

Makes 6 – 10 flatbread, depending on the size

Ingredients

2 Tbsp Olive Oil
3 cups Flour
1 ½ cups Water

Directions

1. Mix all ingredients until dough is incorporated.

2. On a floured surface, take a small ball of dough and roll with rolling pin to form a circle. You may also just use your hands to make a peasant style flatbread.   Add flour as necessary.

3. Par cook in a sauté pan with a hint of olive oil on medium heat about 1-2 minutes on each side.

4. The flatbread can then be refrigerated for several days or frozen for up to 3 months. You can remove the flatbread as needed and thaw.

5. Add your favorite toppings and then bake in a 400 degree oven until crust is golden brown.

Flatbread

Spring roll with dipping sauce

3 • RAW

Vegan Spring Rolls
Makes about 2 cups

If you want to make this recipe 100% raw, you will need to get a raw wrapper. There are many different ones available including seaweed, spinach and hemp. Many in the Raw Community feel that the rice wrapper is acceptable since it is a small part of the overall contents.

Ingredients

¼ cup chopped Scallion, green part only
1/3 cup toasted Sesame Oil
½ cup plus 1 Tbsp Coconut Aminos
½ cup Olive Oil
½ cup Ginger, peeled and rough chopped
1 tsp Coconut Nectar
1 Tbsp Rice Vinegar
Rice Wrapper or Raw Wrapper
Swiss Chard, chiffonade
Kale, chiffonade
Cabbage, grated
Carrot, grated

Directions for sauce:

1. Place toasted sesame oil, coconut aminos, coconut nectar, rice vinegar and ginger in the blender and puree ingredients.

2. Slowly drizzle olive oil in to incorporate sauce.

3. Add salt & pepper to taste.

(Continued on Next Page)

(Continued from previous recipe)

Directions for roll:

1. For the roll vegetables, we use a chiffonade of kale & chard, shredded carrot and purple cabbage. Prepare your vegetables and then toss all the vegetables in a bowl to distribute evenly.

2. Soak your rice wrapper in water, place on flat surface and add vegetables in the wrapper. Top with a drizzle of the sauce. Roll and fold the wrap.

3. Slice and serve with dipping sauce.

Raw Zucchini Noodles
Serves 2

Ingredients

1 large or 2 medium Zucchini grated using a box grater or mandolin into small pieces
2 Tsp Olive Oil
1 Tsp Truffle Oil
5 cherry tomato or sugar plum tomato sliced into quarters
5 Raw Olives quartered
Nutmeat such as raw Sunflower or Walnut
Salt & Pepper to taste

Directions

1. Grate zucchini, using a box grater or mandolin, into small pieces into bowl.

2. Add tomato, olive and nutmeat. Add oil, salt & pepper and toss until thoroughly mixed.

3. Taste for flavor and adjust salt/pepper, truffle oil and ingredients as needed.

Raw zucchini noodles

Chicken noodle soup

4 • SOUP

Making soup is one of Chef Hugo's specialties, and something that he greatly enjoys. His Mother was the family soup maker growing up, as well as the goat cheese maker. He trades recipe ideas with her often. Our soups are healthy, easy and quick to make, something you can enjoy in 1 – 2 hours.

Chicken Noodle

Makes about 12 cups

Ingredients

1/2 Chicken bone in
12 cups Water
1 large Carrot
2 stalks of Celery
½ Onion, sliced
1 ½ oz fresh Parsley
1 Tbsp Olive Oil

Directions

1. Add olive oil and onions to stock pot and sauté until onions are sweated. Add carrot, celery and sauté until soft.

2. Add chicken, parsley and water.

3. Bring to a boil and then reduce to a simmer for 1-1/2 hours.

4. Strain the broth. Separate chicken into pieces and add your favorite cooked pasta or rice.

Creamy Zucchini
Makes about 12 cups

Ingredients

1 Tbsp Olive Oil
2½ lbs Zucchini
½ medium Onion
2 Tbsp chopped Garlic
12 cups Water
2 cups Coconut Milk

Directions

1. Add 1 Tbsp olive oil to soup pan. Add onion and garlic and sauté until garlic is golden and onions sweated. Add zucchini and water.

2. Bring to a boil and then lower heat and simmer for 20 minutes.

3. Add coconut milk and salt & pepper to taste.

4. Blend to combine. Serve.

Squash and Apple Soup
Makes about 12 cups

Ingredients

1 Tbsp Olive Oil
2½ lbs Squash (butternut, hubbard, etc.)
½ medium Onion, chopped
12 cups Water
2 Tbsp chopped Garlic
½ Tbsp Nutmeg
½ Tbsp Cumin
3 Apples sliced and cored, with skin on

Directions

1. Sauté garlic and onion in a pan with olive oil until soft. Add water, squash, nutmeg, cumin and apples.

2. Bring to a boil and then reduce heat to simmer for 30 minutes.

3. Blend all ingredients until creamy.

Creamy zucchini soup

Crispy kale salad

5 • SALAD

Crispy Kale
Makes 1 large salad

This is one of the most unusual salads you will have. The texture should be light and fluffy. This salad was created because of Chef Hugo's love of grilled salads. This is a great foundation salad for protein toppings such as wild salmon.

Ingredients

1 bunch Kale
2 Tbsp chopped Garlic
1 Tbsp Olive Oil
1 tsp Garlic powder
1 tsp black Pepper
Salt to taste
½ Lemon squeezed
Pinch of Red Pepper flake
1 tsp gluten free Breadcrumbs

Directions

1. Tear the kale leaves into large pieces, enough for a bite, into a bowl.

2. Add garlic, salt, pepper and lemon juice. Toss all ingredients several times to coat the kale.

3. Spread out on a baking sheet. Bake in a 400 degree oven for 7 minutes on one side, stir and bake for another 5-7 minutes or until light and fluffy. Remove and let cool for 2 minutes.

4. Place on a plate and dress with Pecorino Romano, a pinch of red pepper flake and breadcrumbs.

Caesar salad

Caesar Dressing
Makes 2½ cups

Ingredients

1/8 cup Coconut Aminos
2 cups of Soy Free Vegenaise
1 Tbsp cup granulated Garlic
¼ cup Lemon juice
1 tsp Dijon Mustard
Salt and white Pepper to taste

Directions

1. Blend all ingredients together.

2. Toss with fresh romaine and tomato, top with pecorino Romano.

Hugo's Honey Lemon Vinaigrette
Makes 2 cups

Ingredients

2½ medium sized Lemons, squeezed
½ cup Honey
½ cup Olive Oil
Salt & black Pepper to taste

Directions

1. Blend lemon juice and honey.

2. Slowly add olive oil incorporate.

To make the salad:

Use equal parts of Kale and Chard
1/8 cup grated Carrots
1 Tbsp dried Cranberry
½ Tomato, diced
1/8 cup Sliced Cucumber
Toss with dressing and top with Signature Crackers (see recipe page 9)

Hugo's signature salad

Chicken and mushroom spaghetti

6 • PASTA

Pasta dishes are a favorite among our customers and Americans in general. People love to tuck into comfort food no matter what time of year.

Chicken & Mushroom Spaghetti
Serves 1

Ingredients

5 oz Chicken Breast, cut into bite-size chunks
4 medium sized sliced Mushrooms
2 Tbsp Garlic
3 Tbsp Olive Oil
1 tsp Red Pepper flake
2 Tbsp Parsley, minced
Salt & Pepper to taste
4 oz of fresh Spaghetti, cooked
1 Tbsp Pecorino Romano

Directions

1. Heat olive oil in pan.

2. Add mushrooms and garlic and sauté until garlic is golden.

3. Add chicken and red pepper flake, salt, pepper, and cook until chicken is done.

4. Add pasta and parsley, toss all ingredients together. Garnish with Pecorino Romano and serve.

Vegetable fettuccine

Vegetable Fettuccine

Serves 1

Ingredients

1 Portobello Mushroom cap, stemmed and sliced
8 oz of your favorite veggies
(we use Carrot, Cabbage, Zucchini, Broccoli, Bell Pepper, Onion)
2 Tbsp Garlic
3 Tbsp Olive Oil
5 oz of fresh Fettuccine, cooked
1 Tbsp Pecorino Romano

Directions

1. Heat olive oil in pan.

2. Add onions, garlic and sauté until garlic is golden and onions sweated.

3. Add veggies and cook for 3 minutes.

4. Add ¼ cup water (preferably pasta water).

5. Cover and cook for 2 minutes.

6. Add salt and pepper to taste, toss with pasta, season again if necessary. Garnish with Pecorino Romano and serve.

Macaroni and cheese

Macaroni & Cheese
Makes about 7 cups

Ingredients

½ Gallon Goat Milk
¼ lb Goat Cheddar Cheese
¼ lb Goat Gouda Cheese
½ lb Goat Chevre
1 tsp Paprika (optional)

Directions

1. Heat milk in a pan. When milk begins to warm, add cheese, rough cut. Stir regularly until all cheese is melted. Add paprika if desired.

2. Simmer for 20 minutes, stirring occasionally.

3. There will be some chunks in the bottom of the pan from the goat gouda. Remove from heat and allow to cool.

4. Place sauce in a blender and blend until a smooth texture is achieved.

5. Prepare pasta.

6. Toss with sauce and enjoy!

Halibut and shrimp with coconut milk cucumber sauce

7 • ENTREES

White Fish with Cucumber Coconut Milk Sauce
Serves 2

Ingredients

2 6 oz pieces of wild white fish such as Halibut, Cod, Rockfish, etc.
1 medium Cucumber, finely diced
1 cup Vegenaise
1 cup Coconut Milk
1½ Tbsp Garlic, chopped
2 Tbsp Parsley, minced
1½ Lemon, squeezed for juice
Salt & Pepper to taste

Directions

1. Sear fish in olive oil on both sides and then finish in a 400 degree oven.

2. While the fish is cooking, make your sauce.

3. Whisk or blend together Vegenaise, Coconut Milk to incorporate. Add garlic, parsley, lemon juice, salt & pepper.

4. Heat sauce in a pan, add cucumbers and when warm drizzle sauce on top of fish. Enjoy!

Chicken marsala

Chicken Marsala
Serves 1

There are two different types of Marsala wine: sweet and dry. You will want to use a sweet Marsala for this dish.

Ingredients

6 oz Chicken Breast, butterflied and pounded
1 Tbsp Olive Oil
3-4 sliced Mushrooms
1½ cups Sweet Marsala Wine
1½ Tbsp Earth Balance
Small amount of flour for coating chicken breast

Directions

1. Heat olive oil in pan. Add mushrooms and sauté for 3 minutes.
2. Dust chicken in flour and remove any excess.
3. Add chicken to pan and sear on both sides.
4. Add mushrooms, Marsala wine and finish cooking chicken until done.
5. Take out chicken and reduce liquid by 75%.
6. Add butter and reduce for another 1-2 minutes.
7. Place chicken breast on the plate, top with mushrooms and sauce.

Port wine rib eye

Port Wine Rib Eye
Serves 1

This sauce is silky and elegant – a perfect pairing for the grass fed beef.

Ingredients

8 oz Grass Fed Rib Eye center cut or Grass Fed Tenderloin
1 Tbsp Olive Oil
1 cup Ruby Port
1 Tbsp Earth Balance
Salt & Pepper to taste

Directions

1. Sprinkle salt & pepper to both sides of the meat.

2. Place olive oil in pan and heat on the stove top.

3. Sear the rib eye on both sides in the pan, and then place in 400 degree oven to cook to desired temperature.

4. In the same pan that was used to cook the rib eye, add ruby port wine and deglaze the pan. Reduce liquid by 75%.

5. Add butter and reduce for 1-2 more minutes. Shake the pan back and forth to incorporate your sauce.

6. Pour sauce on top of beef and serve.

Braised lamb shank

Braised Lamb Shank
Serves 6

This is a hearty, healthy, comfort food dish – perfect for cold winter days.

Ingredients

6 Grass Fed Lamb Shanks
3 medium Onions, large slices
½ bunch Celery, diced large
10 -15 cloves of Garlic
5 large Carrots, cut in half
2 TbspThyme
3 6-inch stalks of Rosemary
1 bottle of Red Wine
3 lbs of diced Tomato
7 oz Tomato paste
Salt & Pepper to taste

Directions

1. Heat oven to 400 degrees. Salt and pepper each side of the lamb shanks.

2. Roast in the oven for 10 minutes on each side.

3. Mix all vegetables, wine and herb ingredients in a large deep pan. When lamb shanks are finished in the oven, place in the pan. Cook in the oven for 2 hours or until meat is tender and falling off the bone.

4. To serve, remove lamb from pan, place on plate.

5. Take some sauce and put it into a sauté pan. Reduce sauce by half and pour over lamb. Enjoy!

Pomegranate cheesecake

8 • DESSERT

Raw Pomegranate Cheesecake   Makes 1 Cheesecake

Both of these dessert recipes are raw and because we use coconut nectar to sweeten them, they are actually healthy desserts. Hard to believe, isn't it?

Crust Ingredients

1 cup raw Cashews
1 Tbsp Lemon Juice
2 Tbsp Vanilla
2 Tbsp Raw Coconut Nectar
¼ cup Coconut Oil

Directions

1. Soak cashews for ½ - 1 hour.

2. Put all ingredients in food processor and blend until incorporated. Layer 9" spring form cheese cake pan with the crust.

3. Freeze base for at least ½ hour.

Filling Ingredients:

3 cups Cashews
½ cup Lemon Juice
1 cup Beet Juice
1½ cup Pomegranate Juice
1 cup Coconut Nectar
1½ cup Coconut Oil
(Continued)

Cacao and avocado mousse

(Continued from previous recipe)

Directions

1. Soak cashews for 1 hour.
2. If using a home sized blender, you will need to blend in 2 steps because the blender will not be able to hold all the ingredients at once. Place ½ of the ingredients in blender and blend, reserving ½ Coconut Oil for the end.
3. Slowly add coconut oil until filling is a smooth consistency.
4. Pour first batch into a large bowl.
5. Repeat the first 3 steps.
6. Pour into a bowl and whisk to combine.
7. Pour into spring form pan on top of crust.
8. Freeze for 2 hours or until frozen.
9. Slice, serve and enjoy!

Raw Cacao and Avocado Mousse
Makes 4-5 cups

Ingredients

1½ cups Coconut Milk
2 Medium ripe Avocados
½ cup raw Cacao
1 Tbsp Vanilla
1 tsp Cinnamon
¼ - ½ cup Coconut Nectar depending on how sweet Avocado is
1 Banana

Directions

1. Start with the coconut milk; add avocado and banana on low speed in the blender. Add remaining ingredients and blend until a smooth consistency is reached.

9 • RESOURCES

Eating a gluten free, soy free, and cow milk dairy free diet is getting easier every day. When our restaurant concept first started, there were quite a few challenges to find the right products that deliver exceptional taste and texture.

Here we share a few of our key foundation resources that we use:

Manini's® Gluten Free Pasta Fresca
Soy Free Earth Balance®
Vegenaise® – Follow Your Heart
Pamela's® Bread Mix
Native Forest® Organic Coconut Milk
Goat Milk
Olive Oil (not extra virgin)
Coconut Secrets Coconut Nectar and Aminos
Ener G Egg Replacer

Questions about the recipes?

Email us at: livehealthyeatorganic@gmail.com
See our videos at: www.youtube.com/hugosorganicrestaurant

Come and enjoy our food when you are visiting Redmond, WA

Hugo's Restaurant
8110 164th Avenue NE
Redmond, WA 98052
425-298-4084
www.hugosorganicrestaurant.com
www.facebook.com/hugoshealthychoice
@hugosorganic on Twitter

ABOUT THE AUTHORS

Hugo Tapa Rodriguez

Born in the small village of Carrillos, Mexico, Chef Hugo Tapia is the youngest of 7 children. He grew up on the family farm, which was in many ways an idyllic life. His parents had pigs, chickens, goats and they grew beans, corn and a variety of other vegetables. His mother also was a cheese maker, making a goat farm cheese that would be sold at market along with other offerings from their land.

As a youth in High School, Hugo enjoyed playing soccer and became quite skilled. He was offered an opportunity to break into the semi-professional world of soccer, but the family lacked financial resources needed to move forward.

After graduating High School, Hugo moved to Mexico City seeking work, which is where he gained his first experience in restaurants. He worked for a family that owned 2 restaurants within 2 blocks of each other. He started as a dishwasher, rapidly progressing to prep cook and sauté. One day the restaurant was short staffed in the front of the house and Hugo was asked to work on the floor waiting tables. His quick smile and easy-going personality were well received by customers, prompting a change to the front of the house. His skill and mastery in the kitchen was quickly missed however, resulting in moving once again, to the back of the house.

After seven years in Mexico City, Hugo and his brother moved to the US. While pursuing work, he drew upon his previous experience and passion of restaurant work. Working in a variety of restaurants for the last 11 years has provided a wealth of knowledge of different styles, techniques, and varieties of cuisine.

As Owner and Executive Chef, he draws upon his farmstead heritage, and a relentless pursuit of creating flavorful and healthy dishes that speak to all the senses, nourishing body and soul.

Teri Sahm

As a teenager, Teri suffered from daily migraine headaches, and came to realize a connection between what you eat and how you feel: you are what you eat! Teri fell in love with the restaurant industry as a young adult. She put herself through college working in restaurants and went on to have careers in the Vocational Counseling industry and Computer Technology industry. However, she found that she kept coming back to restaurants. She has partnered with Hugo to help bring his vision for Hugo's Restaurant to life.

Index

Made in the USA
Charleston, SC
20 February 2017